WHAT'S IN
THE MEADOW?

By Anne Hunter

Houghton Mifflin Company
Boston 2000

www.hmco.com/trade

The text of this book is set in Goudy.
The illustrations are watercolor, colored pencil, and ink, reproduced in full color.

Library of Congress Cataloging-in-Publication Data

Hunter, Anne.
What's in the meadow? / Anne Hunter.
p.   cm.
Summary: Describes birds, mammals, and insects that live in meadows, such as
goldfinches, voles, and fireflies.
ISBN 0-618-01512-4
1. Meadow animals — Juvenile literature. [1. Meadow animals.] I. Title.
QL115.5.H86   2000
591.74'6 — dc21   99-086948

Printed in Singapore
TWP 10 9 8 7 6 5 4 3 2 1

What's in the meadow?

A Woolly Bear Caterpillar

The woolly bear hatches from an egg laid on a plant by a kind of tiger moth. The caterpillar feeds on a variety of meadow vegetation until the time that it pupates, eventually emerging as a tiger moth. Woolly bears can winter in the meadow, curled on the ground, hibernating until spring. They are usually about two inches long.

A Meadowlark

Meadowlarks live in fields and pastures, where they perch on posts and fences to sing their clear, carrying song. Their nests are built on the ground, well concealed by vegetation from predators such as foxes and raccoons. Meadowlarks eat insects, spiders, and seeds, and are nine and a half inches long.

A Spittlebug

The spittlebug is found in the middle of a mass of spitlike bubbles on meadow plants. The pale young insect manufactures these bubbles as protection from drying air and predators as it feeds on plant juices. When mature, the spittlebug will emerge as a small green or brown hopping insect that resembles a tiny frog and is often called a froghopper. Spittlebugs can measure up to an eighth of an inch long.

A Firefly

Fireflies' lights twinkle above the meadow on summer nights. Fireflies, also called lightning bugs, are a type of beetle. The blinking light they use to communicate is created by luminescent chemicals in their abdomens. Adult fireflies live for two weeks to two months and measure from a quarter to three-quarters of an inch long.

A Meadow Vole

Meadow voles are often the most common mammal in the meadow, making tunnel-like runways through the thick grass. Voles look much like mice but are stubbier in shape, with a more rounded nose, flatter ears, smaller eyes, and a shorter, furry tail. Meadow voles eat grasses, seeds, and insects. They measure five to seven inches long. Voles are a favorite food of hawks, owls, and foxes.

A GOLDFINCH

Goldfinches sit like bright jewels atop the meadow's flowers, feeding on their seeds. They have a bouncing ball-like flight and a high musical song. Goldfinches build their cup-shaped nests in the low growth of the field in late summer, laying their eggs when there is an abundant food supply of thistle and other flower seeds. They measure five inches.

A Ladybug Larvae

The spiny, dragonlike larvae of the ladybug hatches from a ladybug egg that is laid on a plant in the meadow. The ladybug larvae feeds on plant aphids and other small insects for two to three weeks before it pupates into an adult ladybug beetle. Ladybug larvae have six legs and measure one-sixteenth to three-eighths of an inch.

A Carolina Locust

The Carolina locust is a kind of grasshopper often found in dry summer fields. When disturbed, the locust bursts up in a short, startling flight, its wings making a loud fluttering rattle. Its call is a buzzing sound made by rubbing its wings together. The Carolina locust feeds on grasses and other plants. It measures one and a half to two inches long.

An Eastern Mole

Moles live under the surface of the meadow. They tunnel through the soil with their wide, shovel-like hands, leaving trails of mounded earth as evidence of their underground passage. Living underground, moles have little need to see and have very poor eyesight, but they have excellent hearing, with ears located beneath their skin. Eastern moles feed on worms, insects, and plants and are five to eight inches long.

A WHITE-LINED SPHINX

There are many kinds of sphinx moths, also known as hawk moths. The white-lined sphinx visits the meadow at dusk, flying from flower to flower to feed on nectar. It has a very fast wing beat, and it resembles a hummingbird in size and speed. A white-lined sphinx has a wing span of two and a half to three and a half inches.

The open, sunny meadow is home to many kinds of sun-loving grasses and flowering plants. These plants provide food and shelter for a great variety of life, from nectar-feeding insects to seed-eating birds and grass-grazing animals. These creatures in turn attract predators such as owls, hawks, foxes, and snakes to hunt. Listen and watch as you walk through a meadow. What is hopping and what is flying, chewing and sucking, tunneling and hunting, singing and buzzing under the warm summer sun?